THE CUTEST ANIMALS OF THE WORLD
Book for Kids

WONDERFUL WORLD OF ANIMALS BOOK 1

JACK LEWIS

The Cutest Animals of the World Book for Kids

Wonderful World of Animals Book 1

Copyright © 2021 by Starry Dreamer Publishing

For information contact:

Starry Dreamer Publishing, LLC 1603 Capitol Ave. Suite 310 A377
Cheyenne, Wyoming 82001
starrydreamerpub@gmail.com

Written by Jack Lewis
Photo Credits: All images contained herein are used under license from Shutterstock.com (See Index for complete list)
Front Cover Photo Credits:
ABB Photo, Richard Seeley, Vladislav T. Jirousek, Lightpoet/Shutterstock
Back Cover Photo Credits:
Vladimir Wrangel, Vladislav 3, Rbrown10/Shutterstock

ISBN: 978-1-952328-58-9 (Hardcover) 978-1-952328-60-2 (Paperback)
978-1-952328-63-3 (Ebook)
Library of Congress Cataloging-in-Publication Data is available
10 9 8 7 6 5 4 3 2 1
First Edition: April 2020

STARRY DREAMER PUBLISHING

Arctic Fox

Arctic Circle

FUN FACT:
THE ARCTIC FOX DOESN'T MIND THE COLD. THEY CAN SURVIVE TEMPERATURES AS LOW AS -58 DEGREES FAHRENHEIT!

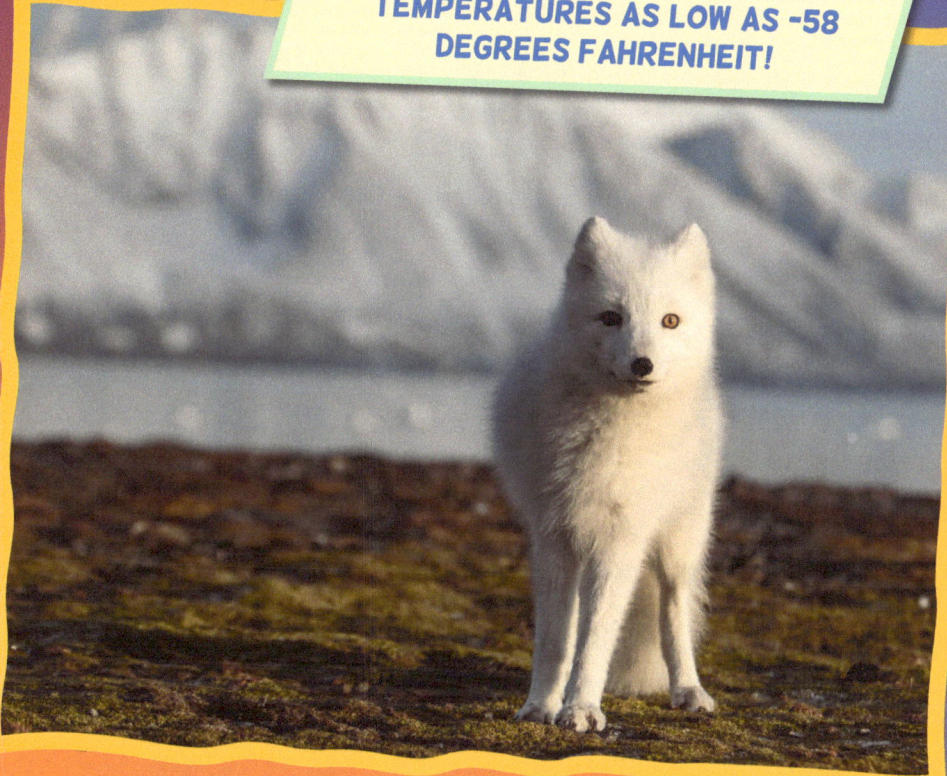

These foxes are fascinating! They can grow their fur to match the color of their surroundings. Sometimes they will follow polar bears to eat the scraps of food the bears leave behind.

QUOLL
Australia and New Guinea

FUN FACT:
A NEWBORN QUOLL IS TINY, ABOUT THE SIZE OF A GRAIN OF RICE!

Sadly, these spotted furry friends are an endangered species. Some people have suggested that quolls should be kept as pets to increase their numbers.

What is an endangered animal species?

An endangered species is a species (population of an animal) that is in danger of becoming extinct. An extinct animal means it would no longer exist anywhere on Earth. Once an animal is extinct, it is gone forever.

How do animals become endangered?

There are multiple reasons an animal species may become endangered. It could happen if it has too many predators, the plants or prey it eats is gone, the places it lives have been destroyed, the climate it lives in changes, or if people overhunt it.

What can I do to help?

Many countries have laws to help protect endangered species, but there are things we can do to save endangered animals and help the conservation of wildlife as well.

- Recycle and reuse items to lessen waste.
- Use non-toxic soaps and cleaners in your home.
- Support an organization that works to save endangered species.
- Visit national wildlife refuges or parks.
- Grow native trees or plants in your backyard or garden.
- Learn about endangered species in your area and teach others about them.

Mandarin Duck
Europe and Asia

FUN FACT:
THE MANDARIN DUCK CAN FLY AS FAR AS 500 MILES A DAY!

Some consider the stunning Mandarin duck to be the most beautiful duck in the world. As a result, they are highly regarded in Chinese culture and are often depicted in Asian art.

Hedgehog

Europe, Asia, and Africa

FUN FACT:
WHEN THREATENED, HEDGEHOGS WILL CURL THEMSELVES INTO A BALL AND USE THE HARD SPINES ON THEIR BACKS AS SHIELDS!

Hedgehogs are some of the most adorable animals on the planet! They make good pets and will spend their time exploring their habitat and chasing (and eating) crickets.

Bottlenose Dolphin

Oceans Across the World

Though they look like giant fish, dolphins are mammals and breathe air as we do. They have blowholes on top of their head they breathe through when they surface. Dolphins are social animals and have interacted with humans in the wild.

Japanese Weasel

Japan

FUN FACT:
LIKE A SKUNK, A JAPANESE WEASEL CAN PRODUCE A NASTY-SMELLING SUBSTANCE TO PROTECT ITSELF!

Japanese weasels may look adorable, but don't let their innocent looks fool you. They are great hunters and use their sensitive noses and ears to find and eat mice and other prey. In addition, they collect grasses or feathers to make their little dens soft and cozy.

Kirk's Dik-Dik

Eastern and Southwestern Africa

These tiny antelopes will hide when they feel threatened. If they're discovered, they will run in a zigzag pattern. Then, they warn others of their kind nearby with a squeaky "dik-dik" sound as they run away.

Slow Loris

Southeast Asia

FUN FACT:
THE SLOW LORIS IS VENOMOUS, AND THEY HAVE A TOXIC LIQUID SPREAD OVER THEIR FUR!

These cute primates live in the dense tree canopies of rainforests, but they can survive in other types of habitats too. Unfortunately, in some parts of the world, people illegally keep them as pets.

American Pika

North America

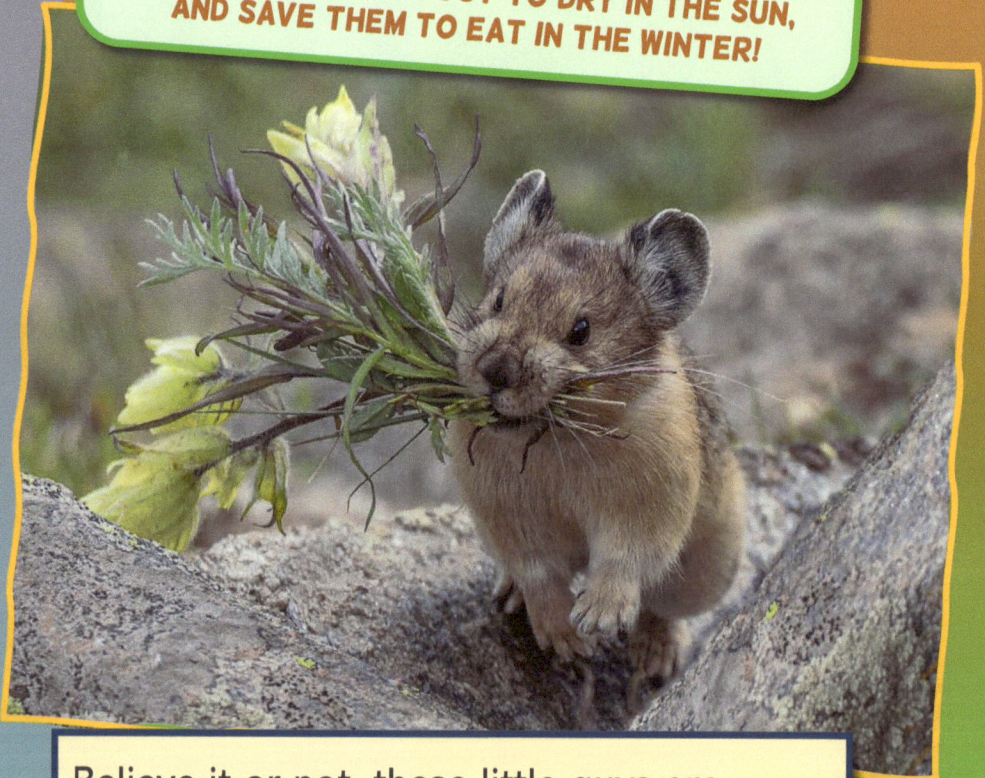

Believe it or not, these little guys are closely related to rabbits. They live in mountainous areas and prefer cooler temperatures. Sometimes they'll steal food from their neighboring pikas. Naughty!

Fennic Fox
Northern and Sub-Saharan Africa

FUN FACT:
WHEN THESE FOXES ARE HAPPY, THEY CAN PURR JUST LIKE A CAT!

Fennec foxes are one of the cutest animals in the world! They live in hot, dry climates, so they mostly sleep in their dens during the day and come out at night. Fennecs can go without water for a while, as most of the moisture they need to survive they get from the plants and animals they eat.

Sunda Flying Lemur

Southeast Asia

FUN FACT:
SUNDA FLYING LEMURS CAN GLIDE OVER 320 FEET AT A TIME!

The Sunda flying lemur is not a true lemur, and they glide rather than fly. They are great at climbing trees but are nearly helpless on the ground.

Numbat

Australia

FUN FACT:
ONE NUMBAT CAN EAT 15,000 - 20,000 TERMITES A DAY!

Numbats use hollow wandoo logs on the ground for shelter and as a source of food. (They eat termites found on the wandoo trees.) Due to the destruction of their habitats and increased predators such as cats and foxes, numbats are now an endangered species.

Sea Otter

Pacific Ocean Coastal Areas

FUN FACT:
SEA OTTERS WILL STORE FOOD OR ROCKS TO CRACK OPEN SHELLS IN POCKETS UNDER THEIR ARMS!

Sea otters are playful creatures found in coastal regions around the Pacific Ocean. They are amazing swimmers and like to float on their backs while they snack on shellfish, starfish, and other sea creatures.

Long-Eared Jerboa

East Asia

FUN FACT:
THE LARGE SURFACE AREA OF THE JERBOA'S EARS DISSIPATES HEAT QUICKLY, SO THEIR BIG EARS HELP KEEP THEM COOL IN HOT WEATHER!

These little critters live in very remote areas of China and Mongolia, so it is hard for scientists to study them. They eat insects and catch them by jumping quickly into the air.

Hummingbird

North, Central, and South America

Hummingbirds love their sweets! These beautiful, tiny birds drink the nectar from brightly colored flowers with their extendible, straw-like tongues. Then, while hovering in the air, they can lick at the sugary nectar up to 13 times per second.

Quokka

Australia

FUN FACT:
IN AUSTRALIA, IT IS ILLEGAL TO TOUCH A QUOKKA, AND IF YOU DID, YOU COULD BE FINED UP TO $2,000!

Quokkas always look so happy! The structure and shape of their mouths make the animals look like they are smiling. Quokkas are marsupials and related to kangaroos and wallabies. A baby quokka lives in its mother's pouch for the first 30 weeks of its life.

Red Panda

Southern and Eastern Asia

FUN FACT:
RED PANDAS CAN SMELL
USING THEIR TONGUES!

The charming little red panda likes to sleep high in the trees during the day. Although they mostly eat bamboo, they will also eat other foods such as acorns, berries, grasses, mice, and birds' eggs.

Javan Tree Frog
Indonesia

FUN FACT:
TREE FROGS EXCRETE STICKY MUCUS THROUGH THE PADS OF THEIR TOES WHICH HELPS THEM CLING TO THE SURFACES!

Pregnant Javan tree frogs will lay their eggs on the leaves hanging over ponds, lakes, or streams. When the eggs hatch, the tadpoles drop into the water below them.

Little Blue Penguin

New Zealand and Australia

FUN FACT:
LITTLE BLUE PENGUINS HAVE MUCH BETTER VISION UNDERWATER THAN ON LAND!

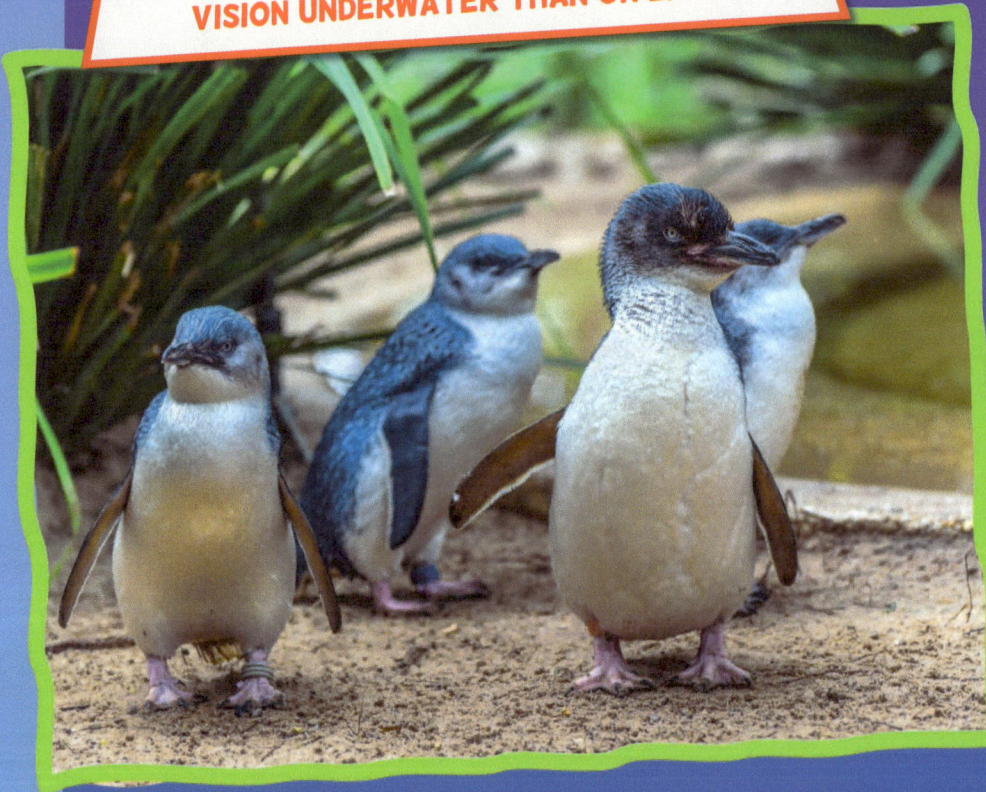

These shy birds are only a foot tall, making them the smallest penguins in the world. They are fast swimmers and very agile in the water.

Patagonian Mara

South America

FUN FACT:
WHEN FRIGHTENED, PATAGONIAN MARAS CAN LEAP UP TO SIX FEET IN THE AIR!

Patagonian maras are grass-grazing animals who can walk, gallop, or hop like rabbits. They can also bounce on all four of their legs in a movement known as "stotting."

Elephant Shrew

Africa

This darling little creature has quite the nose. An elephant shrew will use its long nose to find insects, then flick them into its mouth with its tongue, much like an anteater.

Sand Cat

North Africa, Southwest Asia, and the Arabian Peninsula

FUN FACT:
THE SAND CAT WILL BURY ITS LEFTOVER FOOD IN THE SAND TO SAVE IT FOR LATER!

The adorable sand cat is super shy. Their sandy colored coat is hard to see in the desert environment, and their furry paws don't leave footprints in the sand.

Atlantic Puffin

North Atlantic Coastal Regions

FUN FACT:
BABY PUFFINS ARE CALLED "PUFFLINGS!"

These colorful birds have been nicknamed "sea parrots" or "clowns of the sea" because of the funny way they walk and their brightly colored bills.

Siberian Flying Squirrel

Europe and Asia

FUN FACT:
THE SIBERIAN FLYING SQUIRREL CAN LIVE ITS ENTIRE LIFE IN THE TREES AND NEVER NEED TO COME DOWN TO THE GROUND!

These beautiful squirrels glide rather than fly, and they like to use abandoned woodpecker nest holes for their homes rather than make their own.

Gundi

North Africa

FUN FACT:
GUNDIS HAVE FLEXIBLE RIBCAGES THAT ALLOW THEM TO SQUEEZE INTO TIGHT PLACES TO HIDE!

Looking a little like guinea pigs, gundis are rodents found in rocky desert regions in North Africa. They have good hearing and will warn others in their colony of danger by whistling or thumping the ground.

Chevrotain

Southeast Asia and West Africa

FUN FACT:

THESE DAINTY ANIMALS ARE THE SMALLEST HOOFED MAMMALS IN THE WORLD!

Sometimes nicknamed the "mouse-deer" due to its small size, chevrotains are no bigger than a small dog and not actually deer. Rather than antlers or horns, chevrotains have long canine teeth that look like tiny fangs.

Raccoon Dog

Europe and Asia

FUN FACT:
RACCOON DOGS ARE THE ONLY CANIDS THAT HIBERNATE!

Raccoon dogs aren't actually raccoons but are more closely related to foxes. Although they are cute, they are considered pests in some parts of the world.

Sea Lion

Oceans Across the World

FUN FACT:
SEA LIONS ARE SO FLEXIBLE THEY CAN TOUCH THE TIP OF THEIR REAR FLIPPERS WITH THEIR NOSE!

Sea lions are intelligent creatures known for their playfulness and noisy barking. They use their large flippers for swimming through the sea gracefully, but they look a little clumsy walking on land. They love to eat all types of different fish.

Pygmy Marmoset
South America

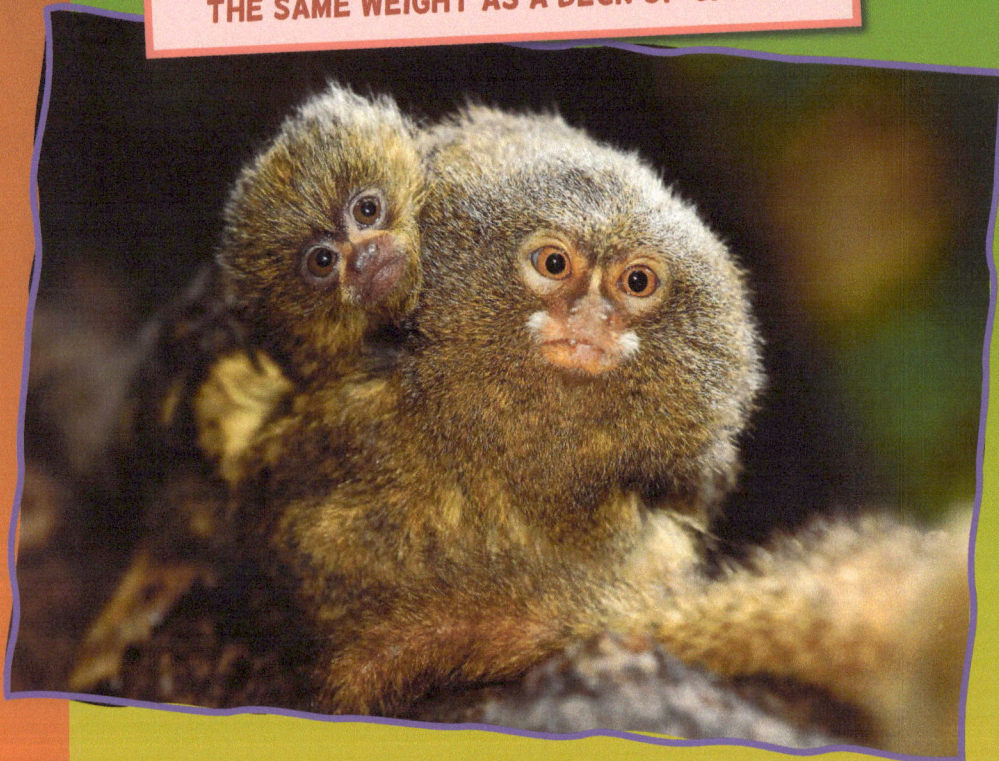

This tiny primate is the smallest monkey in the world. They have sharp teeth to puncture bark and eat gum or tree sap, their favorite food.

Harris's Antelope Squirrel

United States and Mexico

FUN FACT:

THESE SQUIRRELS WILL LIE DOWN AND USE THEIR TAILS AS UMBRELLAS TO BLOCK OUT THE HOT DESERT SUN!

Often mistaken for chipmunks, these fascinating squirrels live in the desert regions of the United States and Mexico. Their diet includes cactus seeds and fruit, mesquite beans, and even insects.

Bongo
Africa

FUN FACT:
BONGOS HAVE BEEN KNOWN TO EAT BURNED WOOD AFTER LIGHTNING STORMS!

Bongos are beautiful antelope found in Central and West Africa. Unlike other antelope, both adult males and females have horns. They like to stay cool by rolling around in the mud.

Serval

Africa

These awesome wild cats have excellent hearing and are good hunters. Servals are bred with domestic cats to create savannah cats, a large cat with dog-like habits that make great pets.

Emperor Tamarin Monkey

South America

These fancy monkeys cooperate and share their rainforest habitat with saddle-back tamarins. Both species help one another out and warn each other of danger.

Ermine

North America, Europe, and Asia

FUN FACT:
ERMINE MALE BABIES ARE
BIGGER THAN THEIR MOTHERS
AT SEVEN WEEKS OLD!

Ermines are small weasels that live in the northern parts of the world. They are excellent tree climbers and move about in a funny zigzag manner. In addition, they can excrete a smelly substance that keeps other ermine away.

Manatee

North and South America, and Africa

The gentle manatee is also known as the "sea cow." It is a mammal that needs to breathe air, but it can hold its breath underwater for up to 15 minutes. It primarily eats seagrasses and plants found on the ocean floor.

Wombat

Australia

FUN FACT:
WOMBATS ARE THE LARGEST
BURROWING MAMMALS IN THE WORLD!

These amusing animals are close relatives of the koala. Wombats are nicknamed "Bulldozers of the Bush." They are fantastic diggers and have built gigantic tunnels and burrows up to 150 feet in length.

Capybara
South America

FUN FACT:
THE CAPYBARA IS THE WORLD'S LARGEST RODENT AND CAN WEIGH OVER 150LBS!

Capybaras are semi-aquatic creatures, meaning they spend a lot of time in the water. They are very trainable and are sometimes raised as pets. Some people call them "giant guinea pigs."

Meerkat

Southern Africa

The charming meerkat is a busy animal. A single meerkat can dig over 400 holes a day and are well adapted to living in the desert. They can close their ears, so the sand stays out, and they have a third eyelid to protect their eyes.

Bushbuck

Africa

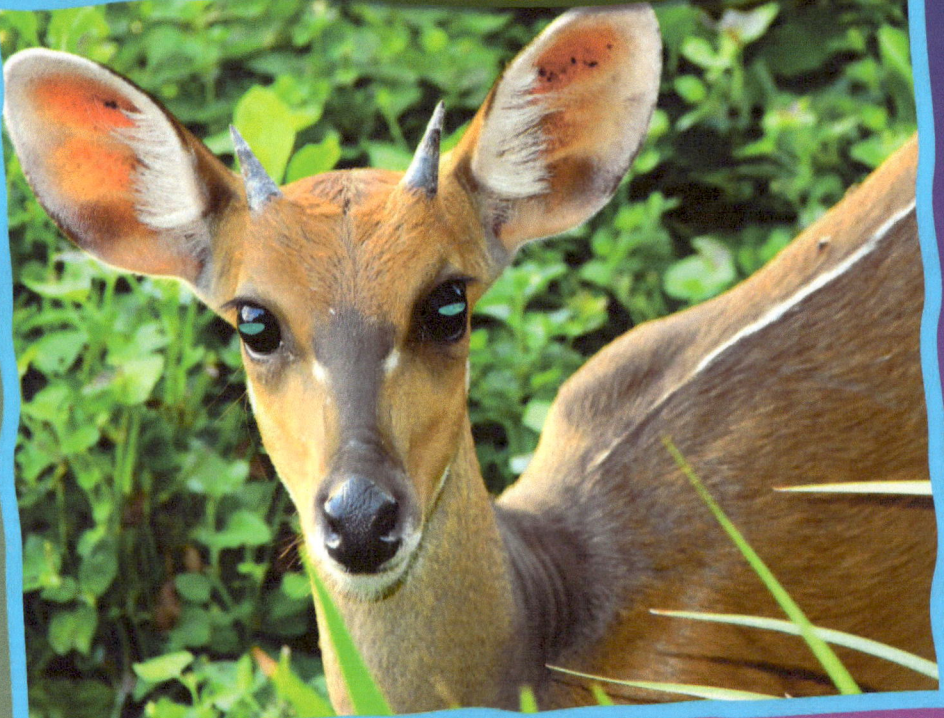

The bushbuck is a graceful African antelope. If they feel threatened by a predator, they may lay flat on the ground to hide, or they may run away while making hoarse barking sounds.

Koala Bear

Australia

FUN FACT:
KOALAS STORE FOOD IN THEIR CHEEKS AND EAT OVER TWO POUNDS OF LEAVES A DAY!

The famous koala is one of Australia's cutest animals. Their name comes from the Aborigine language and means "no water." They rarely drink water and get most of their moisture from the eucalyptus leaves they love to eat.

Tree Kangaroo

Australia and Papua New Guinea

FUN FACT:
WHEN THE WEATHER IS HOT, TREE KANGAROOS
WILL LICK THEMSELVES TO STAY COOL!

Tree climbing kangaroos are fascinating creatures. Rubbery pads on their paws help them climb trees, and they can jump to the ground from heights of 49 feet without getting hurt. They are also the only species of kangaroo able to move or walk backward.

Black-Footed Ferret

North America

FUN FACT:
BLACK-FOOTED FERRETS CAN SLEEP UP TO 21 HOURS A DAY!

The black-footed ferret is the only ferret native to North America. These slim, furry friends are an endangered species, but fortunately, their numbers are slowly increasing.

Guinea Pig

South America

FUN FACT:
HAPPY OR EXCITED GUINEA PIGS WILL REPEATEDLY HOP OR LEAP INTO THE AIR. THIS IS KNOWN AS "POPCORNING"!

Guinea pigs are found all over the world but are originally from South America. Nobody knows where their name comes from as they are not related to pigs and do not come from Guinea in Africa. These cuddly critters make wonderful pets.

Cuban Tody

Cuba

FUN FACT:
THESE BIRDS WILL BURROW AND MAKE A TUNNEL IN CLAY EMBANKMENTS FOR THEIR NESTS!

Small and brightly colored, the Cuban tody is one beautiful bird. This species of tody can be found only in Cuba and the islands surrounding it.

Coquerel's Sifaka Lemur

Madagascar

There are over 100 types of Lemurs in Madagascar, but Coquerel's sifaka lemurs are unique. These lemurs stand on two feet and use their powerful hind legs to leap up to 30 feet in a single jump.

Pudú

South America

The pudú deer is so small that it often stands on its hind legs to reach the plants it likes to eat. Sometimes, pudú will even try and climb trees or bamboo thickets to get at tasty fruit.

Harp Seal

North Atlantic and Arctic Oceans

FUN FACT:
THESE SEALS CAN DIVE UP TO 1,300 FEET BELOW THE SURFACE AND STAY UNDERWATER FOR 16 MINUTES!

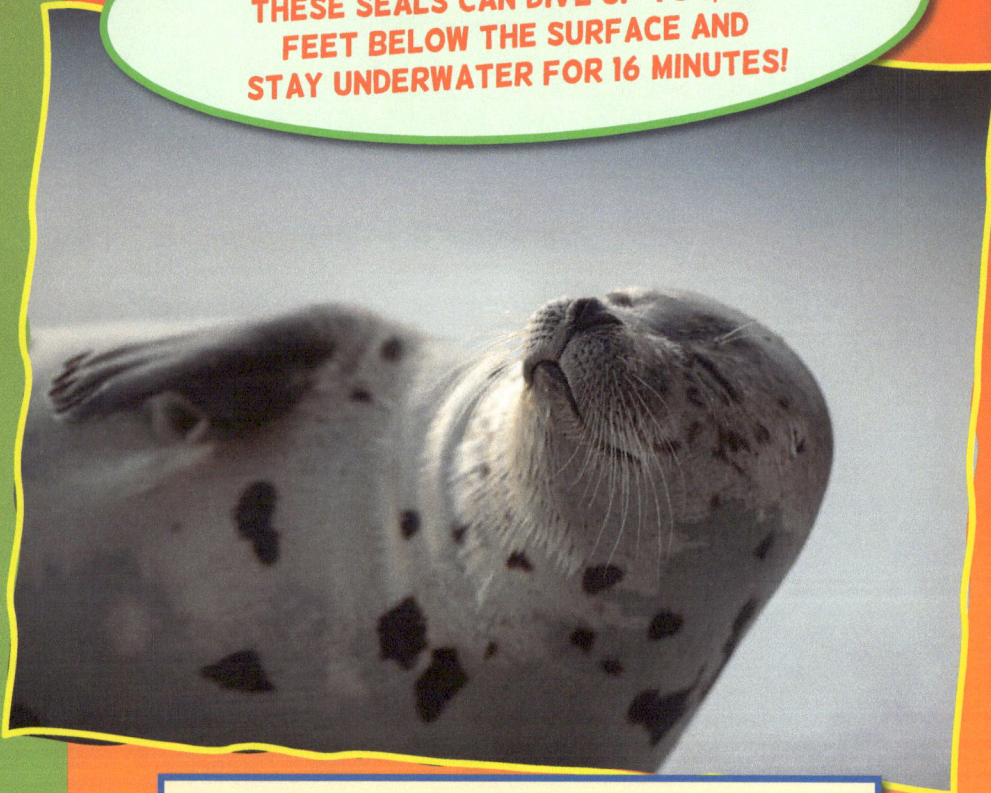

This sweet-looking seal is a delightful creature. Harp seals are amazing swimmers and spend most of their lives in the open sea. They have a thick layer of fat called blubber, which keeps them warm in the frigid waters.

Viscacha

South America

FUN FACT:
EVEN WHEN THEY ARE HAPPY, VISCACHAS OFTEN LOOK TIRED OR BORED!

Viscachas are rodents more closely related to chinchillas rather than rabbits. They thrive in the high elevations of South America and spend much of their day grooming or resting on rocks in the sunshine.

Northern Saw-Whet Owl

North America

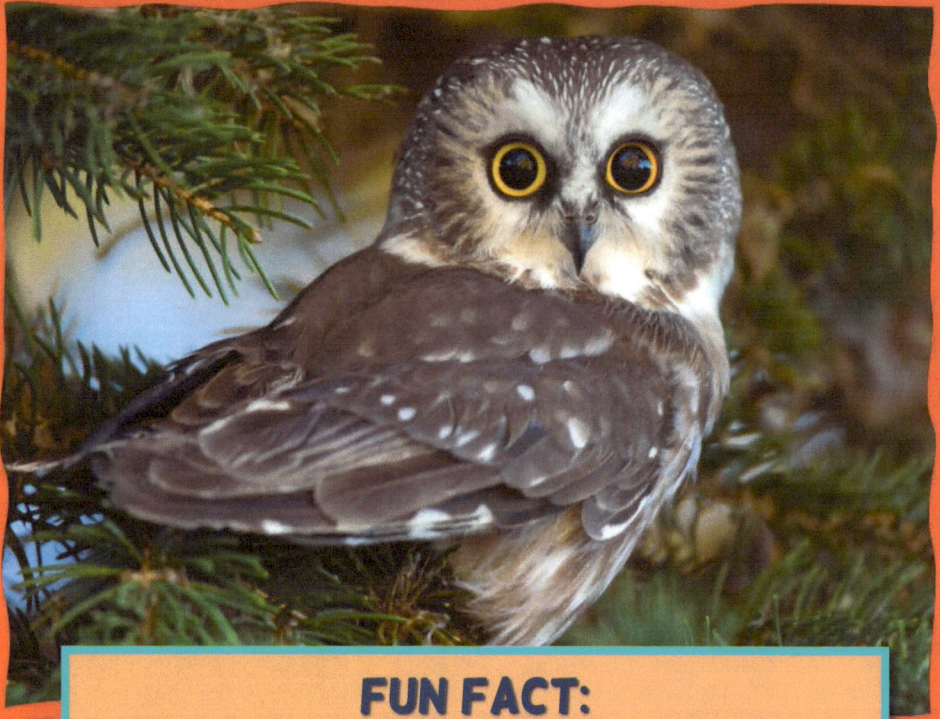

FUN FACT:

WHEN THIS OWL FEELS IN DANGER, IT WILL POSE A WING AND ITS BODY TO LOOK LIKE A TREE BRANCH!

Saw-whet owls are one of the smallest owl species in North America. They are known for making unique "too-too-too" sounds and will sometimes hoot for hours without stopping. Because of their excellent hearing, they can hunt in complete darkness.

Margay
Central and South America

FUN FACT:
MARGAYS CAN CLIMB
DOWN A TREE HEAD-FIRST!

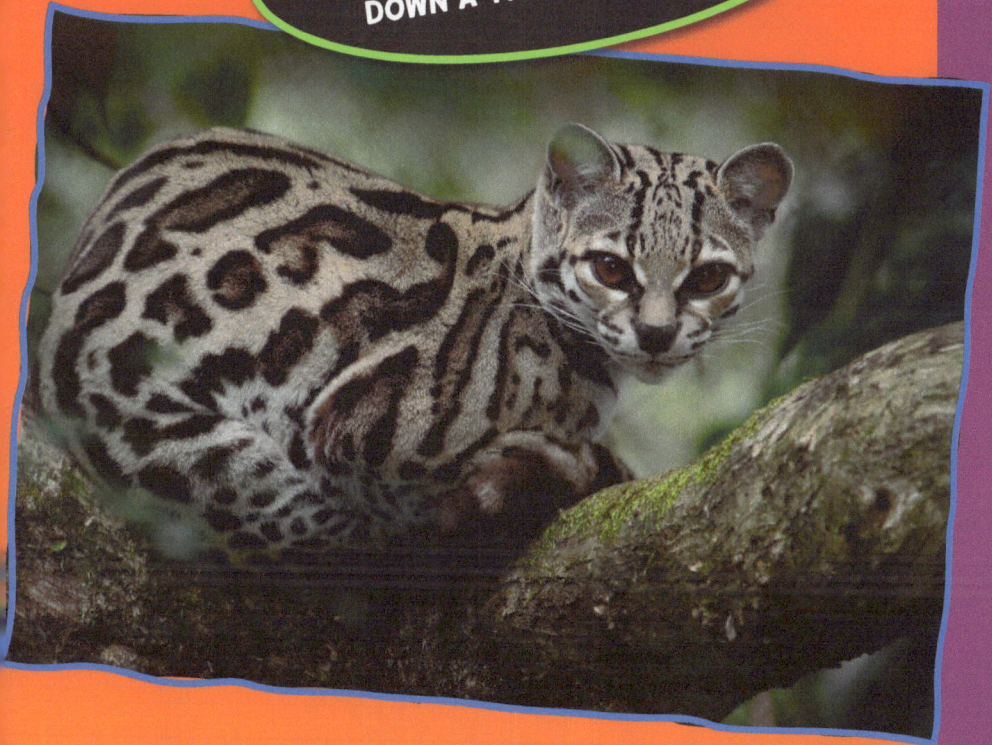

Margays are tree-loving cats found in rainforest habitats. They are excellent climbers and will even make nests and sleep in the treetops.

Gerenuk

Africa

FUN FACT:
GERENUKS CAN STAND UP AND WALK SHORT DISTANCES ON THEIR TWO HIND LEGS!

These amazing gazelles look like they might come from a different planet! Their name "gerenuk" comes from the Somali language and means "giraffe-necked." They will stand on two legs and stretch their long necks to reach food up to 6.6 feet off the ground.

Prairie Dog

North America

This relative of the squirrel is especially adorable. Prairie dogs live in large groups and build huge underground "towns." They make separate rooms for sleeping, eating, nurseries, and even for toilets.

Binturong

Southeast Asia

FUN FACT:
BINTURONGS ARE ALSO KNOWN AS "BEARCATS" ALTHOUGH THEY AREN'T RELATED TO BEARS OR CATS!

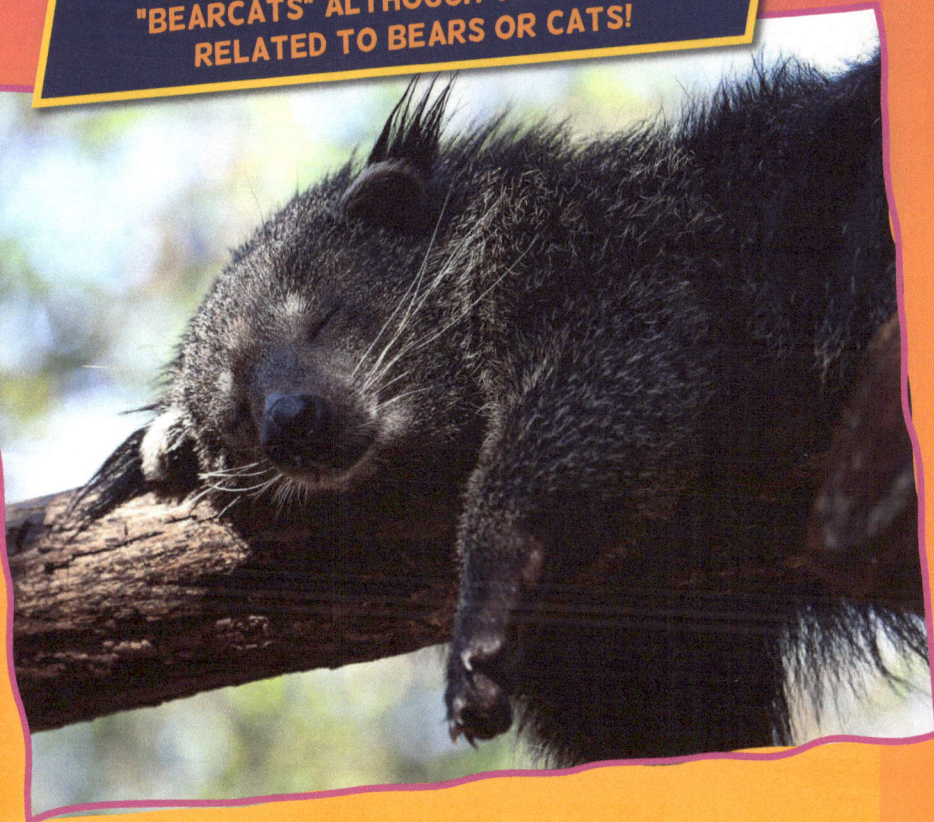

Binturongs spend most of their day in the treetops, either sleeping or slowly roaming while looking for food. They will eat almost anything, but they are especially fond of fruits like figs or bananas.

Red Squirrel

Europe and Asia

FUN FACT:
RED SQUIRRELS CAN FIND THEIR BURIED FOOD UNDER MORE THAN A FOOT OF SNOW!

With tall tufts of red fur on the tops of their ears, these remarkable squirrels are unmistakable. Sadly, only 1 in 6 red squirrels live until their first birthday due to starvation, disease, or being eaten as prey. Red squirrels and their nests are protected under the 1981 Wildlife and Countryside Act.

Sitatunga

Africa

Sitatungas are beautiful antelope found in central Africa. They are well adapted to the water and are skilled swimmers, although they will avoid areas that might have crocodiles.

Streaked Tenrec

Madagascar

FUN FACT:
STREAKED TENRECS ARE THE ONLY MAMMAL SPECIES THAT WILL RUB PARTS OF THEIR BODY TOGETHER TO PRODUCE SOUNDS IN AN ACT CALLED "STRIDULATION" LIKE INSECTS OR SNAKES MAY DO!

These fascinating prickly animals look like a cross between a shrew, a hedgehog, and a porcupine. The spiky quills on its back help protect it from predators. However, when threatened, it will head-butt its opponent.

Chinchilla

South America

Chinchillas are small South American rodents with soft fur. Their fur is the thickest of any animal on the planet. Though they are often sold as pets, their numbers in the wild are decreasing.

Snowy Owl

North America, Europe, and Asia

FUN FACT:
A SNOWY OWL'S HEARING IS SO GOOD THEY CAN HEAR PREY CRAWLING UNDERNEATH SNOW!

These magnificent owls have a dense, soft feather coat that keeps them warm in freezing temperatures and allows them to fly and hunt silently.

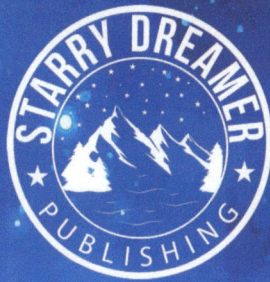

Enjoy these other great books by JACK LEWIS:

Never Bring a Zebracorn to School

Joy to the World: The Best Christmas Gift Ever

Wonderful World of Animals Series

Take a trip around the world to find the wildest, weirdest, and most adorable animals on the planet!

The Cutest Animals of the World

The Weirdest Animals of the World

The Most Dangerous Animals in the World

Today I Found... Series

Magical children's stories of friendship and the power of imagination!

Today I Found a Unicorn

Today I Found a Mermaid

Today I Found an Elf

Fun with Family Series

A wonderful way to celebrate each special person in our families!

I Love My Mommy

INDEX